INSIDE HISTORY

Ancient Egypt

Illustrated by Peter Dennis

W
FRANKLIN WATTS
LONDON • SYDNEY

Contents

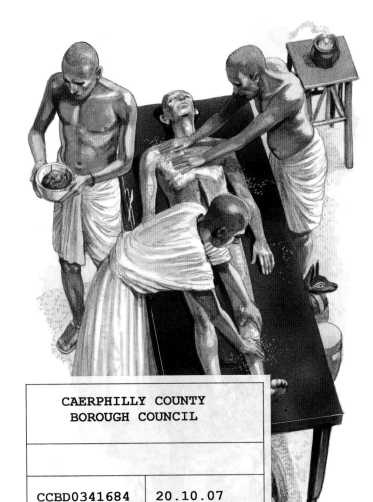

Ancient Egypt

People have lived in the fertile land of Egypt beside the river Nile for thousands of years. Each summer the river floods, coating the earth with a layer of rich mud, ideal for growing crops. It was here, over 5000 years ago, that a great civilization emerged.

The people of ancient Egypt worshipped hundreds of gods and goddesses who represented everything from motherhood and wisdom to the sun, moon, stars and sky. They built great temples to their gods and massive pyramids and spectacular tombs for their kings, known as pharaohs.

The ancient Egyptians believed in life after death. If you had lived a good life, then your soul would pass into the Next World where life was restful for evermore. They preserved the bodies of rich and important people by mummifying them, so that they could come back to life again in the Next World. People were buried with all the things they might need in the Afterlife, including food and clothes and statues of servants to do their work for them. Pharaohs were also buried with gold and treasures.

In this book you can explore inside a pyramid and see how it was built, wander through a temple and come face to face with a mummy in his tomb. Along the way you will meet some of the people who built these amazing structures, and see how they lived.

The pyramid

It is 2500 BC and the pharaoh of ancient Egypt has come to see how the construction of his great pyramid is progressing. Twenty years ago, when he first became pharaoh, he ordered the building of the pyramid to be both his tomb and a lasting monument to his greatness. Now the pyramid is almost finished. Thousands of workers are busily polishing and painting its outer surface made of perfectly fitting, smooth limestone blocks.

BUILDING THE PYRAMIDS

First the plan of the pyramid was marked out on the ground with stakes and string. Priests used the position of the stars to line up the pyramid's four sides so that they faced exactly north, south, east and west. Then the ground was levelled and the pyramid built up layer by layer from giant limestone blocks, like a massive staircase. The blocks were hauled up the pyramid on a ramp built of earth and rubble that spiralled up the pyramid's sides.

CASING STONES

The outside of the pyramid was faced with triangular blocks called casing stones made of a finer limestone than the building blocks. These were levered into place starting at the top of the pyramid and working down to give a perfectly flat surface. They were polished by hand until they were completely smooth.

Workers shave and polish the limestone casing stones.

Workers hail the pharaoh

Passing up supplies

Stepped structure of pyramid

Narrow shaft points directly to the Pole Star

KING'S CHAMBER

At the heart of the pyramid was the burial chamber of the pharaoh. In here his body rested inside a stone coffin, called a sarcophagus, surrounded by treasures and items he would need in the Next World. The weight of the pyramid above the chamber was supported by five solid slabs of granite.

PAINTING AND GILDING

The glowing red of the pyramid stood out against the sands of the desert making it visible for many kilometres. At the very top of the pyramid was a pointed capstone which was gilded— covered in gold—to reflect the sunlight.

SHAFTS AND GALLERIES

As well as the galleries leading to the chambers, there were narrow shafts to the outside for the pharaoh's soul to pass through on its way to the stars.

Closely fitting stonework

Narrow passage lit by torches

Pyramid entrance

Donkeys are used to carry loads

Ramp

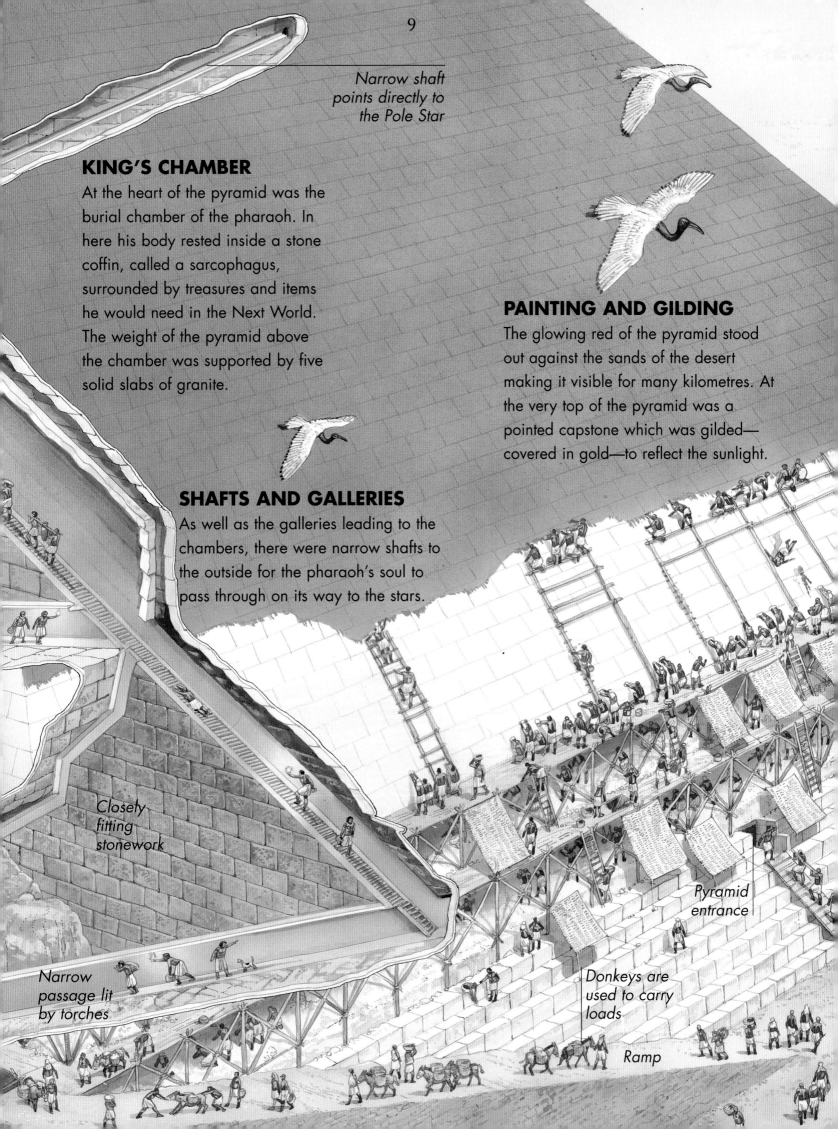

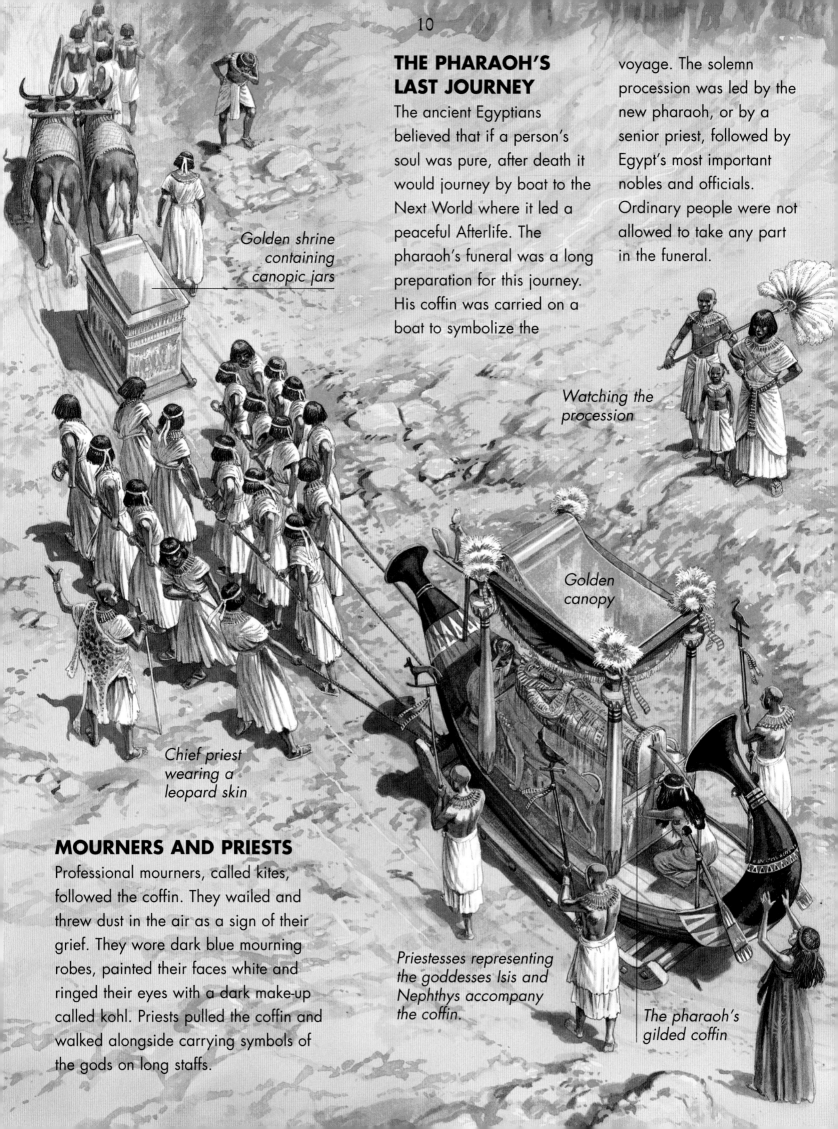

Golden shrine containing canopic jars

THE PHARAOH'S LAST JOURNEY

The ancient Egyptians believed that if a person's soul was pure, after death it would journey by boat to the Next World where it led a peaceful Afterlife. The pharaoh's funeral was a long preparation for this journey. His coffin was carried on a boat to symbolize the voyage. The solemn procession was led by the new pharaoh, or by a senior priest, followed by Egypt's most important nobles and officials. Ordinary people were not allowed to take any part in the funeral.

Watching the procession

Golden canopy

Chief priest wearing a leopard skin

MOURNERS AND PRIESTS

Professional mourners, called kites, followed the coffin. They wailed and threw dust in the air as a sign of their grief. They wore dark blue mourning robes, painted their faces white and ringed their eyes with a dark make-up called kohl. Priests pulled the coffin and walked alongside carrying symbols of the gods on long staffs.

Priestesses representing the goddesses Isis and Nephthys accompany the coffin.

The pharaoh's gilded coffin

INSIDE THE TOMB

Cut deep into the rock, beneath the feet of the funeral party, lay the hidden tomb of an earlier pharaoh, Tutankhamun. Its chambers housed all the goods and treasures that might be needed by the pharaoh in the Next World.

Annexe

Burial chamber

Shrine containing Tutankhamun's coffin

Treasury

Anubis

Shrine

In the Valley of the Kings

Nearly 1500 years have passed since the great pyramids were built. Pharaohs are now buried here, in the Valley of the Kings. The funeral party of a dead pharaoh has just arrived. It has crossed the Nile from the religious city of Thebes to the east, and now progresses slowly to the pharaoh's newly finished tomb. As the procession wends its way through the valley, it passes the tombs of other long-dead pharaohs, all hidden from sight buried deep beneath the rocky ground.

The boat is a symbol of the pharaoh's journey to the Next World.

GOLDEN SHRINE

Shrines in ancient Egypt were containers made of wood, stone or precious metal in which a statue of a god or goddess was kept. They were also used to contain the coffins and canopic jars of important people, particularly pharaohs.

Polishing the gilded decoration on the shrine

PAINTED CHAMBER

Artists adorned the walls with scenes of the pharaoh's funeral and his journey into the Next World. Their last job was to paint the entrance when it was filled in. They left the chamber through an opening in the bottom, which was then sealed.

Wall paintings show Tutankhamun with gods and goddesses.

Tutankhamun's shrine is made of gilded cedarwood, decorated with blue inlay.

Stone sarcophagus

An oil lamp throws light on to the door about to be sealed.

Three more shrines nest within the first shrine, and enclose a stone sarcophagus.

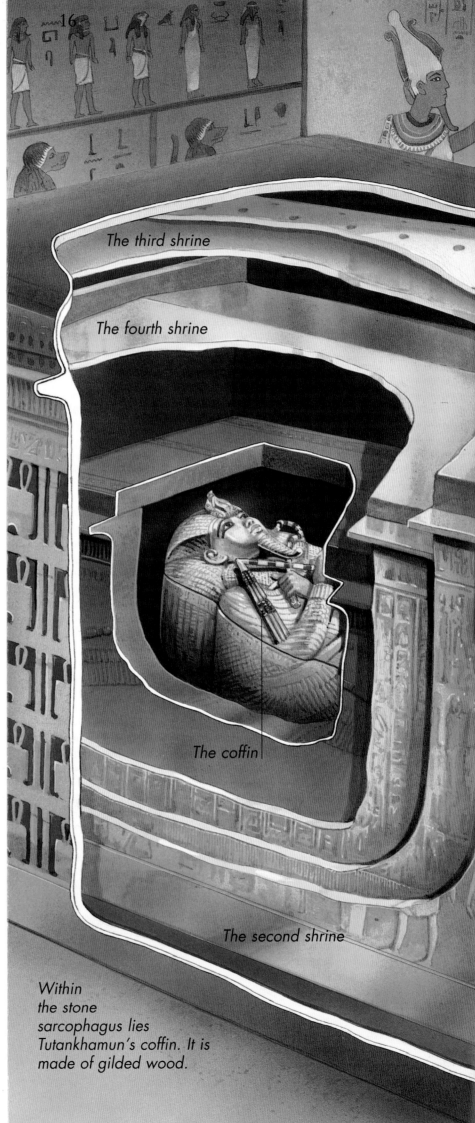

The third shrine

The fourth shrine

The coffin

The second shrine

Within the stone sarcophagus lies Tutankhamun's coffin. It is made of gilded wood.

BURYING THE PHARAOH

The pharaoh's coffin was lowered carefully into its stone sarcophagus. Priests covered it with a linen shroud as they said prayers for the king. The sarcophagus was made of a hard stone called quartzite and decorated with carvings of goddesses Isis, Nephthys, Neith and Selket.

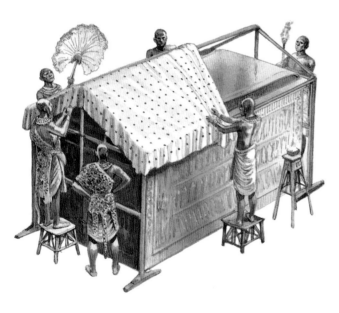

FINAL FAREWELL

Four gilded shrines were built panel-by-panel around the sarcophagus. Just before the final shrine was put in place, the priests erected a wooden frame. On this they hung a linen shroud decorated with spangles to represent the starry sky.

Pharaoh's tomb

Many years earlier, the boy pharaoh Tutankhamun died suddenly, aged only 19. Here, in the burial chamber of his tomb, priests are about to seal the massive gilded outer shrine containing his coffin.

Linen shroud with spangles

Wooden frame to support the shroud

The shrines were assembled inside the chamber itself.

Priests prepare to seal the final shrine.

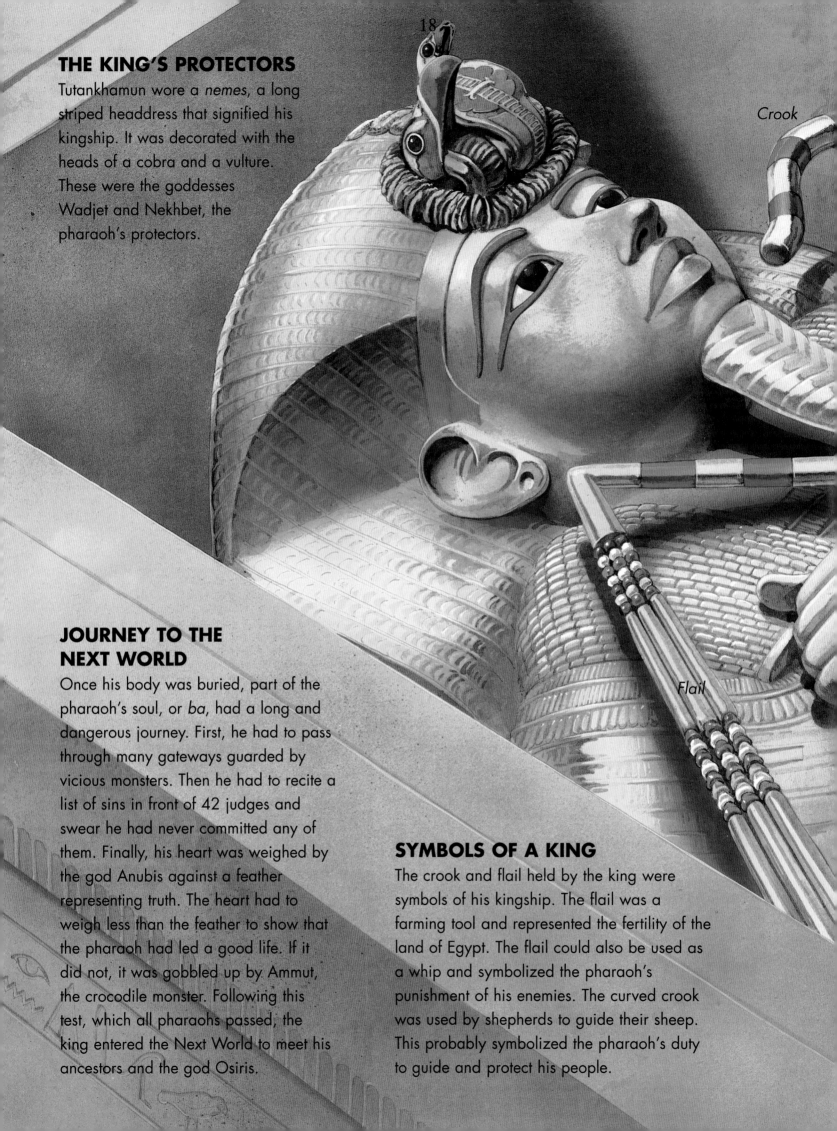

THE KING'S PROTECTORS

Tutankhamun wore a *nemes*, a long
striped headdress that signified his
kingship. It was decorated with the
heads of a cobra and a vulture.
These were the goddesses
Wadjet and Nekhbet, the
pharaoh's protectors.

Crook

JOURNEY TO THE
NEXT WORLD

Once his body was buried, part of the
pharaoh's soul, or *ba*, had a long and
dangerous journey. First, he had to pass
through many gateways guarded by
vicious monsters. Then he had to recite a
list of sins in front of 42 judges and
swear he had never committed any of
them. Finally, his heart was weighed by
the god Anubis against a feather
representing truth. The heart had to
weigh less than the feather to show that
the pharaoh had led a good life. If it
did not, it was gobbled up by Ammut,
the crocodile monster. Following this
test, which all pharaohs passed, the
king entered the Next World to meet his
ancestors and the god Osiris.

Flail

SYMBOLS OF A KING

The crook and flail held by the king were
symbols of his kingship. The flail was a
farming tool and represented the fertility of the
land of Egypt. The flail could also be used as
a whip and symbolized the pharaoh's
punishment of his enemies. The curved crook
was used by shepherds to guide their sheep.
This probably symbolized the pharaoh's duty
to guide and protect his people.

COFFINS WITHIN COFFINS

Inside the first coffin were two more, fitting one inside the other. The second coffin was also made of gilded wood and plaster, and was even more finely decorated than the first. It was inlaid with lapis lazuli, a semi-precious blue stone, and covered with a red and blue pattern called *rishi*. This was based on the shape of feathers and symbolized the soul. The final coffin was made of solid gold. It was also decorated with patterns and semi-precious stones.

Pharaoh's mummy

Inside the stone sarcophagus is a magnificent coffin made of wood and plaster covered with gold. It is beautifully patterned and moulded in the shape of the dead pharaoh's body. He carries a crook and flail, symbols of his kingship, and his face is shown as that of Osiris, prince of the dead.

HURRIED FUNERAL

Tutankhamun died unexpectedly young, aged only 19. Because of this, the preparations for his burial, which usually take many years during a pharaoh's reign, had not yet been made. There was no tomb cut ready for him, and one had to be hastily dug. This might explain why it is smaller than most other pharaohs' tombs. It is also possible that his coffins had originally been made for someone else. His outer coffin was too big to fit into the stone sarcophagus. It had to be shaved down so that the lid would close.

ROOFTOP ROADS

The streets of Deir el-Medina were very narrow and only gave access to some of the houses. Luckily, the flat roofs of the buildings provided another means of getting about. People simply walked across them, using steps and makeshift ladders to climb from one level to another.

OUTSIDE ROOMS

Because the weather was usually hot and dry, roofs and outdoor kitchens were used as extra living and working space. Jobs such as drying fish, washing clothes, cooking and baking were all done outside.

Air vent to direct fresh air into the house

Rich customer visits the carpenter

Drying fish

All the houses are made from mud brick, called adobe.

Playing senet, a favourite game in ancient Egypt

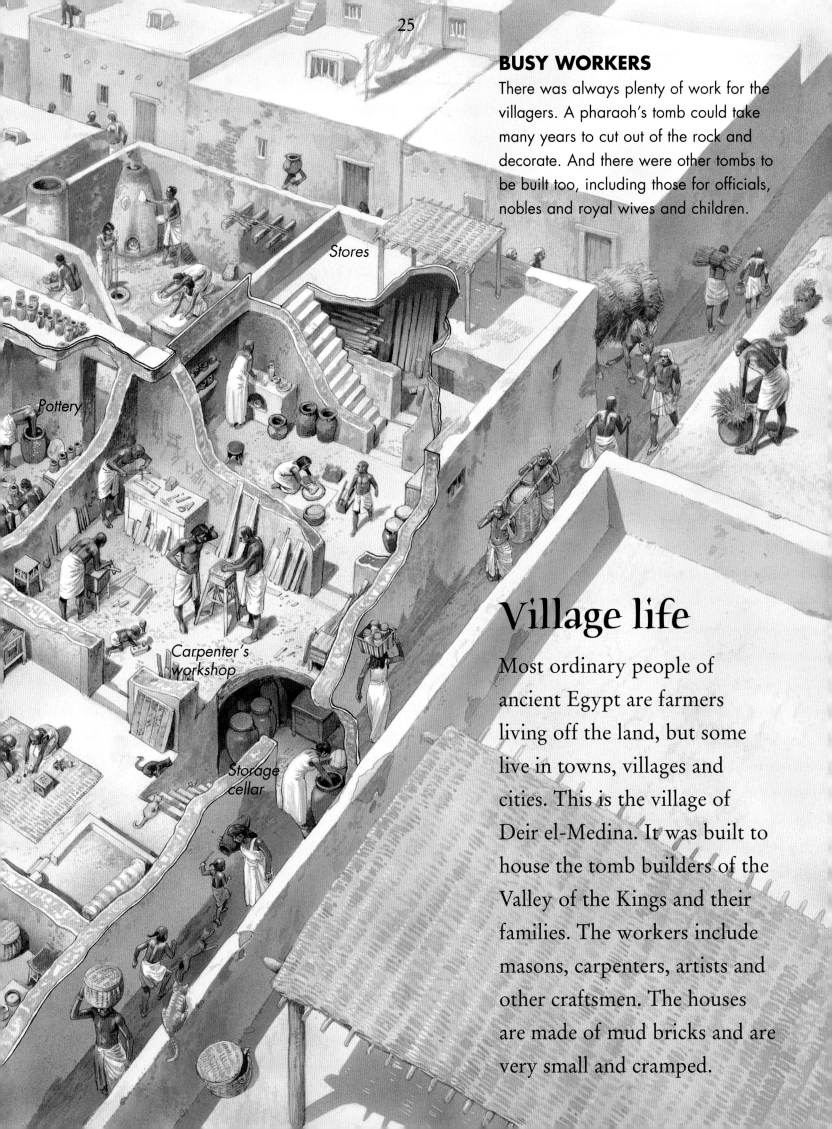

BUSY WORKERS

There was always plenty of work for the villagers. A pharaoh's tomb could take many years to cut out of the rock and decorate. And there were other tombs to be built too, including those for officials, nobles and royal wives and children.

Stores

Pottery

Carpenter's workshop

Storage cellar

Village life

Most ordinary people of ancient Egypt are farmers living off the land, but some live in towns, villages and cities. This is the village of Deir el-Medina. It was built to house the tomb builders of the Valley of the Kings and their families. The workers include masons, carpenters, artists and other craftsmen. The houses are made of mud bricks and are very small and cramped.

AVENUE OF LIONS

These criosphinxes, or ram-headed lions, represented Amun-Re, the chief god of Thebes. Statues of these mythical beasts lined the avenue that led to the main entrance of the temple.

INSIDE THE TEMPLE

Anyone could enter the temple and go as far as the first courtyard, but only the priests, priestesses and the pharaoh himself were allowed to go any further inside. The public areas of the temple were also used for business as well as worship. Gold, ivory, grain and exotic animal skins, such as leopard and lion, were all traded here.

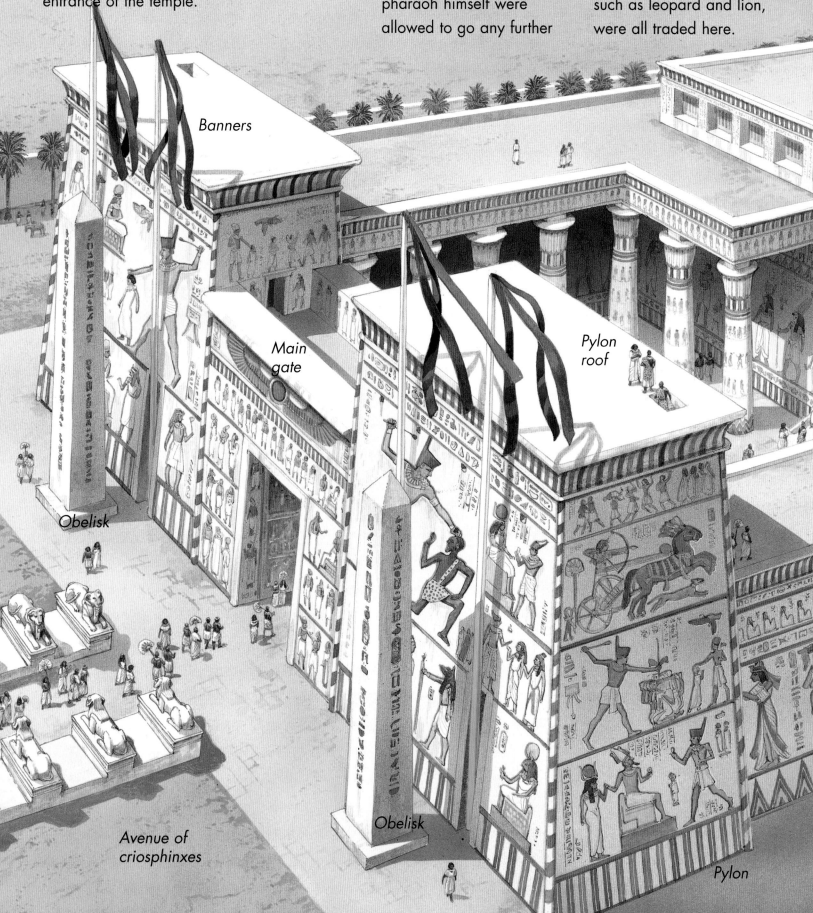

Banners

Main gate

Pylon roof

Obelisk

Obelisk

Avenue of criosphinxes

Pylon

HOME OF AMUN-RE

The ancient Egyptians believed that the god Amun-Re came alive in his statue in the inner sanctuary. Priests woke the statue-god each morning, fed it, clothed it and made offerings to it. Dancers and singers entertained the statue three times a day.

The temple

This great temple is dedicated to the god Amun-Re, the most important god in Egypt and the protector of the city of Thebes. It is built from stone quarried upriver and brought here by boat. It took thousands of labourers and craftsmen many years to build.

Shrine and statue of Amun-Re

Hypostyle hall

Inner sanctuary

Egyptian heiroglyphs (their writing) were carved and painted on the temple walls, along with images of the gods and pharaohs, telling of their heroic acts.

SACRED LAKE

The water in this lake was sacred and pure. It was used to wash the statue of the Amun-Re inside the temple and was offered to him to drink. Priests and priestesses had to bathe in the sacred lake before they could enter the temple.

Glossary

Afterlife Life after death.

Ba The part of a person's soul that was judged by the gods after death before it could enter the **Next World**.

Canopic jars Containers in which a person's organs were preserved as part of the mummification process.

Capstone The topmost stone of a **pyramid**. It was covered in gold to reflect the sun's rays.

Criosphinx A mythical ram-headed lion, symbol of the god Amun-Re.

Crook A shepherd's curved staff, symbol of a **pharaoh**'s kingship.

Embalm To preserve a body from decay by drying it out with chemicals such as **natron**.

Flail A farming tool. Symbol of a **pharaoh**'s kingship.

Hieroglyphs Pictures used to write down the Egyptian language.

Hypostyle hall The large central hall of a temple with its roof held up by giant pillars shaped like papyrus reeds.

Mummy An embalmed body.

Opening of the Mouth A funeral ceremony that gave back the senses and movement to a **mummy** in the **Afterlife**.

Next World The place a person's soul went to after death.

Papyrus A reed used to make paper.

Pharaoh A king of Egypt.

Pylon The gateway to a temple.

Pyramid A massive stepped or pointed building containing a **pharaoh**'s **tomb**.

Sarcophagus A stone outer coffin.

Tomb A burial place cut out of the rock or marked by an elaborate building.

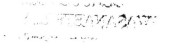